Talking About
Divorce

Nicola Edwards

Chrysalis Children's Books

First published in the UK in 2003 by

Chrysalis Children's Books

The Chrysalis Building, Bramley Road, London W10 6SP

Copyright © Chrysalis Books PLC 2003

ISBN 184138 8262

British Library Cataloguing in Publication Data for this book is available from the British Library.

A BELITHA BOOK

Editorial manager: Joyce Bentley
Senior editor: Sarah Nunn
Picture researchers: Terry Forshaw, Lois Charlton
Designer: Wladek Szechter
Editor: Kate Phelps
Consultant: Dr Ute Navidi, Head of Policy, ChildLine

Printed in China

The pictures used in this book do not show the actual people named in the text.

Foreword

Divorce – and the periods before and after separation – can be difficult enough for adults. Wrapped up in their own problems, often struggling with raw emotions, parents may not notice how sad and confused their children are by what's happening. And children may find it hard to talk to their parents, anxious not to burden them further with their worries.

Talking About Divorce helps adults to listen and children to ask questions and express their views about divorce and separation. Together, they can explore the reasons why parents may decide to go their separate ways and talk about everyone's feelings when they do. That children can go on loving both parents is one of the book's reassuring messages, as well as telling children that divorce is never their fault. Identifying someone who will listen – a trusted adult, a friend of their own age or ChildLine – means taking the first step towards finding help.

Informative and thought-provoking, the **Talking About** series tackles some disturbing aspects of contemporary society: divorce, domestic violence, racism, eating problems and bullying. Adults often try to protect children from these problems or believe they will not understand. Taking children through a series of situations they can identify with – using words and images – also means offering alternative ways of resolving conflict. Each book shows that even very young children are not passive observers or victims but want to make sense of their world and act to make life better for themselves, their families and other children.

Ute Navidi, Head of Policy, ChildLine

Contents

What is divorce?

Divorce is when two people decide they can't live together any more.

When Michael's parents got divorced, Michael felt angry and very sad.

It can take a long time for people to feel happy again after a divorce in the family.

Today many **marriages** end in divorce. People who aren't married can decide to **separate** too. When parents split up, it is sad and confusing for everyone.

Why do people get divorced?

When people get married or set up home together it's an exciting time. But sometimes things don't work out as people hope.

When parents divorce they live apart. So their children have two homes instead of one.

Sometimes when parents argue, they forget that their children can hear them.

Just because couples argue, it doesn't have to mean they will split up.

There are lots of reasons why couples get divorced. They may grow apart and develop interests that they don't share. They may find that they want different things.

Feeling sad and worried

When a mum and dad are **arguing** at home, it can make their children very unhappy.

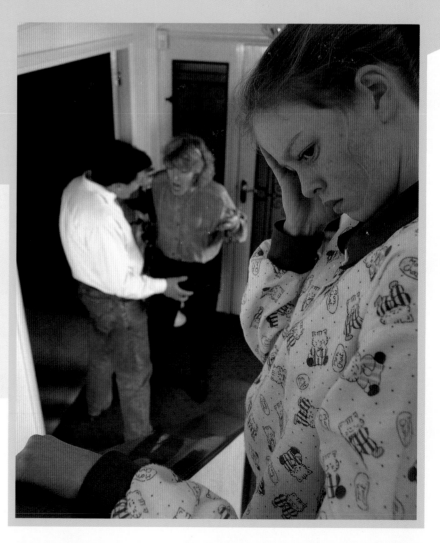

Rachel felt **lonely** and helpless because she couldn't stop her parents arguing.

David told his aunt he was worried about his parents arguing.

Parents can be so wrapped up in their problems they can't see how upset the children are.
It's frightening for children to hear the people they love shouting at each other.

If you are worried about things at home, tell someone you **trust**.

9

The effect on the family

Children worry about their parents splitting up. Very young children often want someone to be with them all the time. They may have trouble sleeping, have nightmares or wet the bed. Older children often feel very angry. They may take this anger out on others by **bullying** them.

Ginny comforted her brother when he had a nightmare about being left all alone.

John bullied his
brother because he was angry.
He didn't want his mum to leave home.

If your parents are splitting up, you don't have to stop loving both of them. They will always be your mum and dad.

Spending time apart

Sometimes a couple decide to have a **trial separation**. This means that one of them moves away from home for a while.

Ravi's dad told him not to worry and that he would see him at the weekend.

Maria missed her mum and wanted her to come back home.

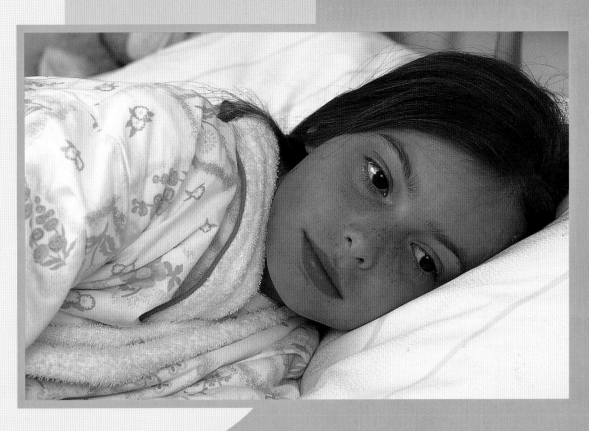

A trial separation gives both people the time and space to think things over and decide what they want to do. This is often a very worrying and upsetting time for children.

Is it my fault?

Children often feel that they are somehow to blame for their parents splitting up. They feel **guilty**. Sometimes they offer to be good if their parents will just get back together again.

Michelle's mum and dad told her she'd had nothing to do with them getting divorced.

But children are not **responsible** for
how a mum and dad feel about each other.

Ruby felt sick
when she thought about
how her mum and dad
were making each
other unhappy.

A divorce is never
the fault of a child.

Mum and dad forever

When a parent moves away from home, children can feel very scared and **confused**. They find it hard to believe their mum or dad really loves them if they can leave them.

Lydia's mum told her that she would always love her.

Danny felt happy and
excited to be with his dad.

Your mum and dad
will always be your
mum and dad.

Children worry that their other parent
will leave too. But when parents stop
being married, it doesn't mean they
stop loving their children.

What's happening?

When parents are splitting up, it can be hard for them to give their children all the care they need.

It helped Pui Chi when her parents explained how things would be different after their divorce.

Joseph talked to his dad whenever he felt worried about anything.

Mums and dads are often upset and worried about the future for their children after a divorce. But it helps children if their parents listen to their views and answer their questions.

It can help people in a family to talk about how they are feeling.

Missing a parent

When parents get divorced it can mean that everyday life changes for everyone. The biggest change is that one home becomes two separate homes.

Jason's mum always sent him a present on his birthday.

Robin rang his dad to tell him he had won a badge at his gym club.

Often after a divorce the children live with one parent for most of the week. They see their other parent every weekend or every couple of weeks.

Children often miss their parent and wish they hadn't left home.

changes

Things can feel strange after a divorce. Children may have to move house and go to a different school. Their mum or dad may have a new **partner** who may have children of their own.

Ryan felt lonely at his new school. He missed his friends.

Sanjay found it hard to **concentrate** at school. He talked to his teacher about how he was feeling.

Children may feel angry with their parents for being responsible for these changes. At home there may be less money to spend on food, clothes or days out.

Time together, time apart

When children see their other parent on the weekend, it gives them a chance to spend time together.

Dan's dad moved in with his new partner and her daughter, Tara. Dan liked seeing his dad and playing with Tara.

Robert felt sad because he didn't see his mum much any more and he missed her.

Don't feel bad about loving your mum and dad equally.

When it's time to say goodbye at the end of a visit, it can be very upsetting for everyone. Children sometimes feel they are being **disloyal** to one parent if they enjoy spending time with the other.

You're not alone

Children whose parents are divorcing can feel unhappy when they see that their friends' parents are still together.

Henry's dad had a new partner but Henry still hoped his mum would come home.

Carly talked to her friend Jo about her parents' divorce. Jo's mum and dad had always lived apart and she was happy spending time with each of them.

Keeping worries bottled up inside doesn't make them go away. Sharing them can help.

But there are children in every school who have been through a divorce in the family. It can help to talk to each other about how it feels. Talking to brothers or sisters or other relatives or family friends can help too.

Feeling happy again

There's no quick and easy way to feel happy again after a divorce. But parents who were sad together can become happier by living apart.

Liam's dad married again. Now Liam has a baby sister.

At first Jane and Ed weren't sure about their mum's new partner. When they got to know him, they liked him a lot better.

It's easier for children to cope with divorce if they know their parents will always love them. Talking about what is happening and how everyone is feeling helps a lot too.

Words to remember

arguing Having a disagreement.

bullying Hurting someone or making them feel sad.

concentrate To give something your full attention.

confused Feeling uncertain and mixed-up.

disloyal Not being true to someone or taking sides against them.

guilty Feeling as if you have done something you shouldn't.

lonely Feeling sad, as if you have no friends.

marriage When two people sign a paper during a ceremony and then live together as husband and wife.

partner Someone who is one half of a couple.

responsible Feeling that something is up to you.

separate To live apart.

trial separation To live apart for a while. After a trial separation, some couples decide to live together again and others decide to get divorced.

trust Feeling that someone won't let you down.

Organisations, helplines and websites

FOR CHILDREN:

ChildLine

A charity offering information, help and advice to any child with worries or problems.
Address for adults:
45 Folgate Street, London E1 6GL
Address for children:
Freepost NATN1111, London E1 6BR
Free and confidential helpline for children and young people: 0800 1111
ChildLine Scotland bullying helpline:
0800 441111
www.childline.org.uk

Children's Legal Centre:

To find out more about children's legal rights ring the Children's Legal Centre:
01206 873820

Lord Chancellor's Department

Publishes a leaflet for children, **Me and my family**, about divorce. It can be found at
www.lcd.gov.uk/family/divleaf.htm

NCH Action for Children

Charity working with vulnerable children and families needing support.
85 Highbury Park, London N5 1UD
NCH website for children and teenagers whose parents are splitting up: www.itsnotyourfault.org

Samaritans

A 24-hour service offering help to anyone who is in crisis.
Helpline: 08457 90 90 90

FOR PARENTS:

Gingerbread

Information and support for lone parent families.
7 Sovereign Close
Sovereign Court
London E1W 3HW
Advice line: 0800 018 4318
www.gingerbread.org.uk

National Family Mediation

Aims to help parents who live apart to remain close to their children.
Star House
104-108 Grafton Road
London NW5 4BD
www.nfm.u-net.com

NSPCC helpline:

Runs a free, 24-hour service offering counselling and advice: 0808 800 5000

Parentline Plus

Offers help, support and information to anyone parenting a child.
Helpline: 0808 800 2222
www.parentlineplus.org.uk

Relate National Marriage Guidance

Counselling organisation aiming to help people to work through their relationship difficulties.
Head Office
Herbert Gray College
Little Church Street
Rugby CV21 3AP
www.relate.org.uk

Index

Picture credits
Front cover (main) Bubbles/David Lane, front cover left to right: Bubbles/Chris Rout, Bubbles/Pauline Cutler, Corbis/Andrea Pizzi, Bubbles/Ian West, 4 Corbis/Jose Luis Pelaez, 5 Bubbles/Jennie Woodcock, 6 Bubbles/Pauline Cutler, 7 Corbis/Andrea Pizzi, 8 Bubbles/David Lane, 9 Bubbles/Frans Rombout, 10 Bubbles/Loisjoy Thurstun, 11 Bubbles/David Lane, 12 Corbis/Ariel Skelly, 13 Bubbles/Jennie Woodcock, 14 Bubbles/Chris Rout, 15 Getty Images/Ron Chapple, 16 Corbis/John Feingersh, 17 Bubbles/John Powell, 18 Getty Images/Kevin Kornemann, 19 Getty Images/David Harry Stewart, 20 Bubbles/Jennie Woodcock, 21 Bubbles/Ian West, 22 Bubbles/Pauline Cutler, 23 Bubbles/Angela Hampton, 24 Corbis/Jose Luis Pelaez, 25 Photofusion/Paul Baldesare, 26 Bubbles/Peter Sylent, 27 Bubbles/Chris Rout, 28 Bubbles/Loisjoy Thurstun, 29 Bubbles/Angela Hampton, back cover Getty Images/Ron Chapple